Watch Plants G

WATCH
TULIPS GROW

By Kristen Rajczak

Gareth Stevens
Publishing

Please visit our Web site, www.garethstevens.com. For a free color catalog of all our high-quality books, call toll free 1-800-542-2595 or fax 1-877-542-2596.

Library of Congress Cataloging-in-Publication Data

Rajczak, Kristen-
 Watch tulips grow / Kristen Rajczak.
    p. cm. – (Watch plants grow)
 ISBN 978-1-4339-4845-9 (library binding)
 ISBN 978-1-4339-4846-6 (pbk.)
 ISBN 978-1-4339-4847-3 (6-pack)
 1. Tulips–Growth–Juvenile literature. 2. Tulips–Development–Juvenile literature. I. Title.
 QK495.L72M395 2011
 635.9'3432–dc22
                                    2010038505

First Edition

Published in 2011 by
Gareth Stevens Publishing
111 East 14th Street, Suite 349
New York, NY 10003

Editor: Kristen Rajczak
Designer: Haley W. Harasymiw

Photo credits: Cover, pp. 9, 13, 15, 17, 23; p. 1 Focus on Nature/iStock.com; p. 3 Michael Rozanski/iStock.com; p. 5 (seeds) Ruud d Man/iStock.com; pp. 5 (bulbs), 11 Hemera/iStock.com; p. 7 Fiona McLeod/GAP Photos/Getty Images; p. 19 Chris Jackson/Getty Images; p. 21 Gay Bumgarner/Getty Images.

Printed in the United States of America

CPSIA compliance information: Batch #CR217260GS: For further information contact Gareth Stevens, New York, New York at 1-800-542-2595.

WATCH
TULIPS GROW

Tulips grow from seeds and bulbs.

Tulip seeds take years to grow.

7

Tulip bulbs grow fast.

The bulb grows under the dirt.

Leaves grow first.

A flower grows at the top.

The flower opens. It looks like a cup.

Tulips can grow where it is cold.

Animals eat tulips. Rabbits eat tulips!

Tulips come in many colors.

23

Words to Know

bulb

seed